From the first time I heard Katherine speak about her Inner Essence Project, I was inspired and intrigued. I loved the simple, practical and deeply meaningful approach to finding a way to live a happier, more fulfilling life. I am so happy that Katherine has decided to write this book in order to share her Project and ideas with the world. This kind of positive and uplifting approach is so very needed and presented in a format that is easy to apply to our lives. Thank you, Katherine!

–Cindy Novelo
Founder and Owner, Breathe Live Love Music and Life Coaching

"Living from Your Heart: The Inner Essence Journey" is a rare combination of mind/body techniques you can read, understand...then actually USE to make wise changes in your life.

–Linda L. Moore, Ed.D
Psychologist... author of Release from Powerlessness: Take Charge of Your Life

In order to change our lives and unleash our full potential, we must be willing to take inspired action. Inspired action and attitudinal shifts are key to bringing about the life we are created to have and enjoy.

In her book, Katherine uses simple, yet profound ideas and action steps to facilitate this process. A powerful guide to lasting change and love unleashed!

–Reverend Darlene Strickland is an ordained Unity minister and spiritual teacher. Currently serving as the Senior Minister at Unity of the Blue Ridge in Mills River, North Carolina.

LIVING FROM YOUR
HEART

THE INNER ESSENCE JOURNEY

KATHERINE A. DASTA

BALBOA
PRESS
A DIVISION OF HAY HOUSE

Copyright © 2017 Katherine A. Dasta.

All rights reserved. No part of this book may be used or reproduced by any means, graphic, electronic, or mechanical, including photocopying, recording, taping or by any information storage retrieval system without the written permission of the author except in the case of brief quotations embodied in critical articles and reviews.

Balboa Press books may be ordered through booksellers or by contacting:

Balboa Press
A Division of Hay House
1663 Liberty Drive
Bloomington, IN 47403
www.balboapress.com
1 (877) 407-4847

Because of the dynamic nature of the Internet, any web addresses or links contained in this book may have changed since publication and may no longer be valid. The views expressed in this work are solely those of the author and do not necessarily reflect the views of the publisher, and the publisher hereby disclaims any responsibility for them.

The author of this book does not dispense medical advice or prescribe the use of any technique as a form of treatment for physical, emotional, or medical problems without the advice of a physician, either directly or indirectly. The intent of the author is only to offer information of a general nature to help you in your quest for emotional and spiritual well-being. In the event you use any of the information in this book for yourself, which is your constitutional right, the author and the publisher assume no responsibility for your actions.

Any people depicted in stock imagery provided by Thinkstock are models, and such images are being used for illustrative purposes only.
Certain stock imagery © Thinkstock.

Print information available on the last page.

ISBN: 978-1-5043-7660-0 (sc)
ISBN: 978-1-5043-7662-4 (hc)
ISBN: 978-1-5043-7661-7 (e)

Library of Congress Control Number: 2017903743

Balboa Press rev. date: 04/06/2017

DEDICATION

To Lidia, Nishta, LeLiya,
Mai Ly, and Abel

CONTENTS

Dedication v

Preface ix

Part I: Stop Behaviors 1

    Chapter 1: Wanting 3

    Chapter 2: Holding 7

    Chapter 3: Assuming 11

    Chapter 4: Monitoring 15

Part II: The Five Essential Laws of Life 19

    Chapter 5: The Law of Intent 21

    Chapter 6: The Law of Possibility 25

    Chapter 7: The Law of Choice 29

    Chapter 8: The Law of Giving 33

    Chapter 9: The Law of Trust 37

Part III: Your Body 41

    Chapter 10: Connecting to Your Body 43

    Chapter 11: Your Chakras 53

Part IV: Conclusion 71

    Final Note from Katherine 72

    History of the Inner Essence Journey 73

Part V: Affirmations, Quotes, and Prayers 75

Suggested Reading 83

About the Author 97

PREFACE

I created this program to guide people who want to live a more loving and compassionate life from their Essence. This journey will guide you through making healthy choices, even on those days when your healthy behaviors seem to have taken a vacation.

Throughout this book, I will use male and female pronouns randomly. I also use "God", "Spirit", and "Universe" interchangeably. Please select the one you are most comfortable with or insert another word you prefer.

Take your time reading this book. Let it soak in. I hope you mark all over the margins with your personal notes and keep this book close at hand so you can refer to it when needed. You may want to read through it without doing the activities and then read it again when you have time to do the activities.

The Inner Essence Journey is one of love and compassion that targets long-term results. It works with your inner Self: your Essence.

You will learn four Stop behaviors that will help you recognize the unhealthy actions, which create suffering and interfere with the creation of a healthy self. These are behaviors that you all do at some time or another: wanting, holding, assuming, and monitoring. WHAM is a good acronym to use to remember those behaviors. These do not come from your Essence; they come from fear, and when you stop them, your life aligns with your true Essence. You can often tell if your behavior is an unhealthy Stop behavior by being aware of your body when you are doing the behavior (or even when you think about it). If there is pain and discomfort, then it's a Stop behavior. Sometimes, you can also just stop and ask your self, your Essence, if this is a healthy or unhealthy behavior.

In part II, you will learn the five Essential Laws of Life, which will help you choose healthy behaviors. Finally, in part III, you will learn how to treat your body as a critical part of your Essence. You will learn how to listen to your body and how to balance and clear your energy centers (also known as chakras).

I would like to thank Kelly Rettig for creating the Inner Essence Project with me. Without her creativity and commitment to living and teaching the Essence Journey much of this book would not be possible.

PART I
Stop Behaviors

WHAM! It feels like something punched you in the gut. You've been trying to improve your emotional, spiritual, and physical self, but suddenly, the unhealthy parts of your personality are in charge. It happens to all of us. We may say, "This is too hard," or "Who do I think I am?" or "My life is a mess," or "At this point, there's no way I can change my life." Yet there is a way to get back on your path to a healthier and happier life. Take that feeling like a punch in the stomach and give it a punch right back with Your Inner Essence.

You need to continue your commitment to yourself and say WHAM to the parts of your personality that don't want you to live in your Essence. Your Essence lives from your heart. If you are already following a practice to help you live from your healthy self, you can continue with whatever program you feel is working for you, but include the Inner Essence Journey as its foundation. It will only add to your existing program. If you are not following any practice now, try the Inner Essence Journey on its own. It may be all you need.

CHAPTER 1

Wanting

"Healthy surrender means allowing yourself to 'be' rather than being in a constant state of want."

—Bryant McGill

Paul has been in his same clothes for three days. He has slept most of the time. He feels hopeless and worthless. For as long as he can remember, he wanted to attend a certain college and study medicine. He has been intensely planning to get into this college for the last year. Three days ago, he heard that he did not get accepted. The pain and disappointment were so powerful that his life has been turned upside down.

Wanting is a Stop behavior. It is fine to want things or want something to happen. It becomes a Stop behavior when you suffer if you don't get what you want; your happiness and emotional state becomes affected. When these wants don't happen, feelings of hopelessness, worthlessness, sadness, and anger or depression often occur.

Wanting is one of my most common Stop behaviors; I must constantly recognize it and make a different choice. Sometimes, it is as little as wanting a new piece of jewelry or as big as wanting a certain job. Other times, it is wanting someone to act differently at work or home. I am a mother of three, and wanting has been a common Stop behavior for me. My children are all over the age of twenty-one, but I still want them to behave or think a certain way. I become angry, upset, or judgmental if I don't get what I want. Also, I generally feel pain somewhere in my body when I am wanting from an unhealthy part of my personality. When I catch myself wanting, I stop and look at the five Essential Laws of Life to find a way to change my judgmental, angry, or unhealthy parts of my personality to my Essence of love. You will learn about the five Essential Laws of Life in part II.

Here are some common examples of wanting that I have seen in myself or others: wanting someone to like you, or wanting an A on a paper for a class. Remember, it's healthy to want these things. But it is not healthy to let your wants dump you into despair, self-loathing, or depression. It's how you react when you don't get what you want that shows you which of these wants are healthy behaviors and which are Stop behaviors.

Activity for Wanting

Watch yourself for a few days, and make a note of things you want and how you react when they do not happen. We will come back to this activity later and examine what and where you feel pain in your body.

Unmet Wants   Results/My Behaviors   Where Do I Feel It?

1. I want my daughter to go on a walk with me. / Feeling unloved/ Stomach
2. _____
3. _____
4. _____
5. _____

After you examine your wants and behaviors, circle the behaviors that are unhealthy wanting behaviors. We will come back to those and make a different choice later when we learn the five Essential Laws of Life.

You may want to make notes below about anything you notice regarding your Stop behavior of wanting. At the end of each chapter on an unhealthy behavior, there is an affirmation. Say this affirmation when you are stopping a wanting behavior.

Affirmation: "Today is a good day, and I can do this."
—Louise Hay

Chapter 2

Holding

*"In the end
these things matter most:
How well did you love?
How fully did you live?
How deeply did you let go?"*

—*Gautama Buddha*

Peggy is sitting at her desk, staring off into space. She dabs at her eyes and sniffles. Grant, her boyfriend of four years, broke up with her two weeks ago, and she can't seem to get past it. She knew it was going to happen, and if she were being honest with herself, she thought it was probably for the best. But she kept holding on to the relationship. It was comfortable and something she could count on. Now that he ended it, she feels sad, lonely, and worthless. Her holding on to the relationship was a Stop behavior because it caused her so much pain.

When you hold on to people, thoughts, or things so tightly that you will suffer if you must let go, this is a Stop behavior. You often hold on even though you know you should let go. The fear of the unknown is greater than the pain you will feel in that relationship or job, or the stress of not earning enough money to make the car payments each month. That discomfort is at least familiar.

Megan holds on to plans she has made. When her plan is changed, she gets angry, frustrated, and often judgmental. Her neck and shoulders feel tight and hurt.

Some of us hold on to expectations of people. I expect family and friends to be totally honest with me. When someone doesn't tell me the truth, I get angry and feel betrayed. My teeth clench and my jaw gets sore. I feel pain in my heart area. That discomfort and pain indicates my holding on to this expectation is a Stop behavior.

I know people who hold on to jobs they don't enjoy. Though the job feels secure, they aren't happy with their work. This unhappiness spills over to the rest of their lives. I hear people say that they would love to quit their job and do something else, but the fear of the unknown is too strong. The risk of losing the security is too scary. This is a Stop behavior of holding if that person is unhappy or feeling pain or causing pain to others because of the job. Symptoms of this Stop behaviors include headaches, stress, tension in the back, and digestive issues.

Many of us hold on to jewelry, cars, or homes. They often bring a false sense of worth and security or a connection to a person or event. However, when you lose that thing and experience pain and prolonged suffering, then it is a Stop behavior. If you hold on to everything, you won't have a free hand to embrace the next gift.

Activity for Holding

Spend some days looking at what you hold on to that causes you pain if you lose it. List the behavior of holding and then explain how you react. Try to imagine letting go of what you are holding on to. Where in your body do you feel the pain?

What Are You Holding? Reaction/My Behaviors? Where Do I Feel It if I Lose It?

1. <u>My position at work</u>   <u>Scared and insecure</u>   <u>Lower back</u>
2. _____
3. _____
4. _____
5. _____

> *Affirmation: "I accept life as it is. I do not judge; I do not dramatize. I let life's events come freely, and I welcome the lessons they convey. I stop struggling now. I let go and know that God always gives me that which is most appropriate for my soul."*
>
> *—Author unknown*

CHAPTER 3

Assuming

"Your assumptions are your windows on the world. Scrub them off every once in a while, or the light won't come in."
— *Isaac Asimov*

Diane is walking down the grocery aisles, wondering how much longer she can buy these foods for her family. She just lost her job, and her savings is dwindling. As she pushes her cart, the pit in her stomach is painful. Her legs are weak, and her breathing is labored. How will she provide for her family? Diane assumes that she will not get another job; darkness and fear take over.

People often make unhealthy assumptions. When a dedicated worker doesn't get a promotion she was counting on, she might assume that she will never get a promotion or believe her boss doesn't think she's good enough. Feelings of jealousy, worthlessness, and anger might appear because of that assumption. Some people assume that without a college education, their child won't be as happy or as successful. That Stop behavior can cause lots of conflict, pain, and worry for the parent and the child.

Some people assume that people of certain nationalities or races are dangerous or evil. Assumptions like that cause serious suffering and pain.

I have caught myself assuming that my daughter's life as a single mother will be difficult. This assumption is a Stop behavior because worry, judgment, and all kinds of suffering usually occur, and there is no truth to it. In fact, she is doing well and is quite happy.

A sibling who is missing an item may assume that his brother or sister took it. This assumption prompts arguing, conflict, and pain.

Assuming can actually create the negative situation that you hoped to avoid. If you assume you do not have enough money, you are creating a future where you will not have enough money. Instead, think that you will have all you need. There are many authors who show you how your thoughts create your future. Pam Grout's book *E^2: 9 Do-It-Yourself Energy Experiments That Prove Your Thoughts Create Your Reality* shows experiments to prove how powerful your thoughts can be.

This Stop behavior often has a trigger. Maybe you saw something that triggered an assumption. Sometimes, it's as simple as reading an article about the economy, and then assuming your money isn't safe where it is. Or maybe you notice your neighbor's child can ride a bike, but your child is still on his tricycle. You might assume that your child is behind. There are so many triggers for assumptions.

Activity for Assuming

Notice your assumptions. Be aware of where you feel them in your body, and most importantly, write down what triggered the assumption. That will tell you a great deal about your Stop behavior of assuming and help you prevent actual assumptions.

Below, write your assumptions, their triggers, and where you feel the pain in your body.

Your Assumption   What Triggered It?   Where Do I Feel It?

1. If I say I disagree with my co-worker, he will be mad at me. / Staff meeting/ Throat
2. _____
3. _____
4. _____
5. _____

> *Affirmation: "I let go of my assumptions and can clearly see the truth in my experiences! I release stress for what it is: false assumptions! I let go of the negative assumptions I have."*
>
> *—K.G. Stiles*

CHAPTER 4

Monitoring

"The reason we struggle with insecurity is because we compare our behind-the-scenes with everyone's highlight reel."
—Steve Furtick

You probably know the stereotype of the nosy neighbor who is constantly monitoring everyone on the block. Well, we each have a little of that person in us. We monitor ourselves, our families, our colleagues, and more.

Monitoring becomes a Stop behavior when it causes you or others pain and suffering. You might monitor yourself to see if you have enough money or enough connections in your social networks. You might monitor your children to see if they have the right kind of friends. You can literally spend the entire day monitoring yourself and others.

In the past, I would find myself monitoring whether people liked me. I was very uncomfortable if I thought someone was unhappy with me. As I practiced living from my Essence, I realized what I was doing. So, I noticed when that Stop behavior crept into my mind, and I stopped and became aware of the discomfort I was feeling. Noticing you are doing a Stop behavior and scanning your body to become aware of what you are feeling is a very key step to your Inner Essence.

It's fine to watch for something, but when monitoring causes conflict within yourself and in others, it is a Stop behavior. You can notice situations and act to prompt changes, but you must not be attached to the outcome to the point where you are suffering if it doesn't happen.

Activity for Monitoring

Write down what you are monitoring and where you feel any pain or discomfort in your body while you are monitoring.

I'm Monitoring   **Where Do I Feel It?**

1. My partner's time on the Internet/Chest area

2. _____
3. _____
4. _____
5. _____

You may notice one Stop behavior and realize you are really doing other Stop behaviors as well. Situations can trigger wanting, holding, assuming, and monitoring. For example, you want a new watch but don't have enough money for that specific watch. You monitor everyone's watch and notice who has the watch you want. Every time you see it on someone's wrist you feel a pit in your stomach and clench your jaw. You were wanting and monitoring.

Evan has his 3-year-old daughter every other weekend. She gets angry and upset if he doesn't buy her what she wants at the store. He is wanting her to behave. He is also assuming that everyone in the store is thinking he is a bad father. Evan was wanting and assuming when his daughter started crying in the store.

As you do these activities, remember: Identifying your Stop behaviors is the first step in making healthy changes. Don't beat yourself up or feel ashamed about them. You can't change them if you don't see them.

Identifying your Stop behaviors is very important with your Inner Essence journey. Now that you can see your unhealthy behaviors and stop them, you are going to learn what to do next.

Affirmation:

I will not monitor myself and others. I will let go and trust.

PART II

The Five Essential Laws of Life

The five Essential Laws of Life will guide you toward healthy behaviors. They are the Law of Intent, the Law of Possibility, the Law of Choice, the Law of Giving, and the Law of Trust.

CHAPTER 5

The Law of Intent

"Your thoughts not the world cause your stress."

—Wayne Dyer

Everything we say and do has an intention behind it. Some of our intentions are related to Stop behaviors. Other intentions come from our hearts or Essence. Those intentions relate to healthy behaviors. Make sure your intentions come from your Essence. One way to do that is to ask if your words or behavior will cause pain and suffering for you or others.

It is important to know your intentions. If your intention is associated with Stop behaviors, do not do it. If your intention comes from love, it will prompt healthy behaviors. You may need to check your intentions throughout the day. As you practice identifying healthy and unhealthy behaviors, it will become easier and easier.

I became proficient with looking at my intentions when my children were in their teens. I would stop myself often and ask, "What is my intention?" For example, I might ask my daughter if she was going to wear those shorts in public. Of course, she was going to wear them in public; she was on her way out the door. My intention was triggered by wanting her to wear something else. But I stopped myself from saying anything. What she was wearing was perfectly fine for her generation.

However, there are times when you need to say or do something to protect your children from harm. That is a fine line, but when asking what your intention is, it becomes clear as to when that is a healthy intention. Your body can also help you discern if an intention is related to a Stop behavior. If you are feeling pain and discomfort when doing or saying something, your intention is probably not healthy.

Eric was angry when he saw a woman dump her trash in the parking garage of their apartment instead of using the dumpster. He took a picture and posted it on the apartment community bulletin board. It caused the woman a great deal of stress and embarrassment, not to mention the anger that arose from others in the building. Eric's intention did not come from his Essence; it came from anger. If his only intention was to have her stop dumping the trash in the parking garage, he could have talked to her privately. There would not be any pain or embarrassment, and he would have had the same results.

Paul and Janice were going through a divorce. It was a difficult time for both. Paul filed for custody of their son. He knew he could not be a single parent, but he was angry and scared. His intention was to make Janice upset and scared, too. Once his intentions came from his Essence, they agreed upon joint custody, which was best for everyone.

When looking at your intentions, you may see that many of your behaviors and words are Stop behaviors. When you realize that your intentions cause unhealthy behaviors, you need not to follow through.

Activity for the Law of Intention

Look over the Stop behaviors you wrote about in the activities for chapters 1, 2, 3, and 4. Then select a few and write what your intentions were for those behaviors.

_____

_____

_____

_____

_____

Affirmation:

> *I will be aware of my intentions and stop any behaviors that come from wanting, holding, assuming, or monitoring. What I say and do will come from my Essence.*

CHAPTER 6

The Law of Possibility

"Create in your mind a vision of what you want and NEVER take your eyes from it, and the entire Universe WILL cooperate with it."

—*Abraham-Hicks*

Anything is possible. With intent from our Essence, we have unbounded potential. Young children practice this Law of Life every day. They believe that they can be or do anything. They believe they can be the president, fly a plane, climb the tallest mountain, and so on. As we grow up, our awareness of the Law of Possibility begins to diminish. We need to recover that belief.

Years ago, I read a book called *Psycho-Cybernetics: A New Way to Get More Living Out of Living* by Maxwell Maltz. It scientifically explained the power of visualization and manifesting what you want. So I practiced. I imagined going to work every day in a certain school and teaching a class. I even pictured which classroom. I practiced every day. I graduated and got a job in that school, and my classroom was in that very room I had imagined.

I did this again forty years later when I wanted to move to the ocean. I imagined my day and every detail living near the ocean. Today, I am typing this book sitting in front of my window, looking out at the Atlantic Ocean.

Your Reality Manifesting: The Secret behind the Law of Attraction by Alexander Janzer shows how we can manifest whatever we want. Tony Robbins said, "Before the mind can work efficiently, we must develop our perception of the outcomes we expect to reach. Maxwell Maltz calls this Psycho-Cybernetics: When the mind has a defined target, it can focus and direct and refocus and redirect until it reaches its intended goal."

Your dreams and goals come from your Essence and help you reach actualization. If you visualize making a lot of money so you can make others feel bad, then it will not happen. If you dream that you will make a lot of money and do great things with it, then I believe it will happen. If you want to get a promotion so you can buy a new car for the family and take a family trip, practicing the Law of Possibility will support you in reaching that goal. Every time you wish or want, you change the future. Anything is possible.

Activity for Possibility

You will do this activity before going to sleep. When you are lying in bed, imagine what your life will be like in three to five years. Literally create a movie in your head of the life that you want. Start at the beginning of the day. You are waking up. Where are you? Who are you with (or are you alone)? Visualize the place you live. Is it a house, an apartment, or a condo? Contemporary or old? Then see yourself beginning your day. Do you eat breakfast? What do you eat? Where are you eating? What are you wearing? Where do you work? What do you do? Create a movie of a day in your life. Include all the details: weather, colleagues, friends, car, city or country, and so on.

As you play this movie, you will eventually fall asleep, and part of your brain will remember this. Throughout the next days, you will draw things and people to yourself that will help you reach this dream. Go ahead. Give it a try. It's much more fun than lying in bed and thinking about tomorrow's tasks.

Nothing limits us except ourselves.

Jot down parts of your ideal day:

_____
_____
_____
_____
_____
_____
_____
_____

Affirmation:

I am supported by the limitless Universe in all that I need.

CHAPTER 7

The Law of Choice

"It is never too late to change the direction that your life is going in."

—Wayne Dyer

You always have a choice. With every act and decision, you have a choice. You have a choice to participate in gossip or to get up and leave. You have a choice to buy those expensive designer shoes or to find a pair that is within your budget. You have a choice to help the person in the car that is stopped in the middle of the street or to drive by it. You have a choice to think your life is terrible, or you can choose to see the blessings in your life.

Realizing that you have choices makes you responsible for each of your thoughts and actions. You can't blame others. When you notice you are in the middle of Stop behaviors, you can listen to your Essence and make a different choice. This helps you get out of the Stop behavior and on the path of love and compassion. Louise Hays says, "No matter where we live on the planet or how difficult our situation seems to be, we have the ability to overcome and transcend our circumstances."

I assumed I couldn't be a writer. I had never published anything before; I had not studied writing or taken any writing classes. My ego kept telling me I wasn't good enough. But I finally turned to the Law of Choice. I could continue believing that I was not a writer, or I could choose to write and see what happens. Well, as you can now see, making a different choice allowed me to let go of that old fear.

A friend of mine once asked her father if he liked his job. He said it didn't matter because he didn't have a choice. I believe if he practiced the Law of Choice, he would have had a job he loved.

Sometimes, it's easier to stay in an unhealthy and unhappy relationship because it is familiar. You may not feel happy or joyful anymore. You might actually be unhappy, angry, and distant; you may feel unloved. You could turn to the Law of Choice and do something differently. You could go see a therapist (alone or with your partner), you could ask for a separation, you could get a divorce. You could also choose to stay in the relationship just the way it is. Either way, it is your choice.

We all need to own our lives and the choices we make. Each choice you make affects your future. Make choice from your Essence and you will be happier and more peaceful.

Activity for the Law of Choice

Look deeply and honestly at yourself. Think of a time when you did not own your choice. Maybe you quit a job and blamed others. Or you always wanted to live in the mountains but never did. You made a choice to stay where you are and not move to the mountains. Perhaps, you bought a new pair of shoes you liked. When you got them home, you realized they were a little big, but you kept them anyway. You made a choice to buy the shoes, and you made a choice to not return them. Or you made a choice to laugh along with others at an inappropriate joke when later, you wish you didn't.

Write about some choices you made that were not from your Essence:

_____

_____

_____

_____

_____

_____

_____

_____

_____

Next, look at your life. What triggers Stop behaviors for you? Write them down, and next to them, write down what choice you're going to make from your Essence from now on. Remember: Doing nothing is a choice and can be a choice from your heart.

_____

_____

_____

Affirmation:

Today, I choose joy.

CHAPTER 8

The Law of Giving

"We make a living by what we get, but we make a life by what we give."

—*Winston Churchill*

What you put out into the world comes back to you. Practice the Law of Giving, especially when your Stop behavior is holding or wanting.

Giving is a very powerful Law of Life to practice. A kindergartner was pushing to be first in line out to recess. His class was practicing the Inner Essence Project for Classrooms. His teacher asked him, "What law can you practice to stop the behavior of wanting?" He thought about it and said, "I could give." He let the person behind him be first in line. Then, it felt so good, he let the next person go in front of him, and on and on. He was the last one to leave and came out of the door with a big smile on his face. Giving can be that simple.

When I am holding on to my money and fearful of not having enough, I give some to others, and more comes back in love and as money. The joy of giving is priceless.

At work, Steve had information that helped him make more sales. Rob, his colleague, asked how he made so many sales. Steve was tempted to hold on to his technique, but he was practicing his Essence and chose to share the information with Rob. The minute he shared the information, he felt good. There was no pain or discomfort in his body. Since then, Steve and Rob have helped each other at work.

Joan was on her way home from work. She was tired and anxious to get out of the highway traffic and get home. Joan drove down the highway scowling, wanting to get home fast. Another car tried to merge in front of her; she honked her horn loudly and sped up to block the car. Joan shouted at the driver of the other car and was even more stressed for the rest of the drive. Her intentions were from wanting and holding. She felt discomfort in her jaw and arms. The next time she drove home, Joan decided to take some deep breaths and come from her Essence. When someone tried to merge in front of her, she let them in. She felt good about giving that person space to get on to the highway, and she had a more pleasant drive home.

If you find yourself doing one of these Stop behaviors, that might be a good time to give.

Activity for Giving

To practice the Law of Giving, look back at the holding behaviors you listed in the activity in chapter 2. How could you use the Law of Giving to overcome these behaviors? Write down your action steps. You can do this with any of the Stop behaviors.

_____

_____

_____

_____

_____

_____

_____

_____

_____

Affirmation:

> *"Everything I give to others is a gift to myself. As I give, I receive."*

> —*Author unknown*

CHAPTER 9

The Law of Trust

"Trust that your soul has a plan and even if you can't see it all know that everything will unfold as it is meant to."

—*Deepak Chopra*

Go with the flow and enjoy the journey. I turn to this law of life quite often. Trust that everything is perfect for that moment. Our society encourages us to plan and act. We are rarely urged to wait and trust. But often, if we stop wanting and holding and let go, everything will be fine. We were taken care of for the first nine months in the womb, and we need to trust that we will be taken care of for the rest of our lives.

A woman I knew lost her job and wanted the job back. She was holding on to the belief that this was the best job for her. Later, she found a new and better job. This job had better hours, better pay, and health insurance for her and her family.

Monica was a woman who naturally trusted Spirit. She woke up every morning and believed that whatever happened that day, it would be perfect. She was a joy to be with because her actions and words were from her heart. When she was diagnosed with cancer and told she only had one year left, Monica embraced that diagnosis and trusted that this was her path. She lived each day to the fullest. She transitioned the day after her first great-grandchild was born, and she said she felt so blessed to have met him. Now that is trust.

It's very difficult to truly trust all of life's events, but every time you can let go and trust just a little, then more and more of your life will be free of Stop behaviors; it will be much more delightful. When you can have those moments of pure trust, your life can be rich and full of your Inner Essence.

Activity for Trust

Write down the Stop behaviors that get in the way of your trusting:

1. _____
2. _____
3. _____
4. _____
5. _____

Affirmation:

> "I trust in divine timing. The Universe always has my back."
>
> —*Sarah Prout*

PART III

Your Body

When you are on your Inner Essence Journey it is critical that you are aware of your physical body. Your body tells you so much about what your Essence needs to grow and expand.

CHAPTER 10

Connecting to Your Body

Your body is the temple of your Essence. It is important to know what your body needs and what it is telling you through different feelings and sensations. There are three important actions you can take to know your body better: breathing, stretching, and listening to your energy centers (chakras).

Cleansing Breath: Place your hands on slightly bent knees. Inhale deeply through your nose. Exhale forcefully through your mouth, bending forward to force the air completely out of your lungs. Repeat three to six times.

Below are some routines to help you connect with your body and open your energy centers. You can do these any time you find is best. It's best for me to do them in the morning before I start the day.

These stretching routines can help you become more connected to your body. If you already have an activity such as yoga or Tai Chi, continue that activity and be mindful of your body. If you would like a simple practice that you can do daily, follow the one below.

First Routine: Breathe

Connecting Breath: Stand and close your eyes. Breathe (through your nose) deep into your belly. Your diaphragm pushes out, and your abdomen expands. Breathe into your ribcage, feeling the back of your body expand as well as the front. Finally, feel your collarbones rise as you breathe into the upper lobes of your lungs.

Second Routine: Stretch

Always work within your own range of limits and abilities. If you are pregnant or recovering from any injuries, check with your doctor before practicing these stretches.

Half-Moon and Fingers to Toes

These poses are an excellent way to begin your stretches and your day. They help your spine to be flexible and loose to help your energy flow through your body.

1. First, entwine your fingers and completely lock your arms; make sure your arm muscles are flexed.

2. Lift your hands upwards (above your head) and make sure your entire body points toward the sky.

3. Bend at your hips to the right and to the left, with your arms extended, to loosen up your spine. Do it slowly.
4. When you feel fairly loose, keep your arms raised and bend to the right as far as you can, forming a half-moon. Hold it for a count of ten (or as long as you can), and then come up and point toward the sky. Make sure you are looking forward, and your head is at your elbows.

5. Then, do the same to the left. Bend as far as you can, forming a half-moon. Come up and continue this for ten half-moons.

6. Come up to the pointing-to-the-sky position, bring your head back, and then let your arms and body follow, bending backwards (while taking care that the bend should happen across the length of your entire spine, not just at the hips, as the latter could result in an injury). Make sure your elbows are next to your head. Hold for five to ten seconds (or as long as you can). Then come up to the pointing-to-the-sky position.

7. Now, bend forward, keeping your knees locked, and try touching your toes. The more you do this, the closer to your toes you will get. Eventually, you will touch then with a flat hand.

   The goal here is to bring your torso as close to your legs as possible while keeping your knees locked in and as straight as possible. Stay there for a count of five to ten and come up to the pointing-to-the-sky position.

8. Do steps six and seven four more times.

Half-Knee to Chest

1. Lie on your back with arms and legs extended.
2. Exhale and draw your left knee to your chest, clasping your hands around your knee.
3. Hold for up to a minute.
4. Then, do the same with your right knee. Do this for at least four times each knee.

Knee to Chest

1. Stay on your back, exhale, and draw both knees to your chest.
2. Clasp your hands around your knees (or as close as you can) and keep your back flat on the floor.
3. Breathe and hold for up to one minute or as long as you can.
4. Exhale; extend both legs and arms to rest on the floor. Repeat up to five times.

Living from Your Heart The Inner Essence Journey

Cobra

1. Lie face down on the floor or a mat, with the tops of your feet flat on the mat.
2. Press into the floor with both hands, with palms slightly lower than your shoulders. Spread your fingers and press into the floor.
3. Pull shoulders back and away from your ears.
4. Tighten your abs by pulling your belly button toward your spine.
5. Lift into the cobra pose, using your back and abdomen.
6. Hold five to ten seconds and gently release.
7. Repeat two more times.

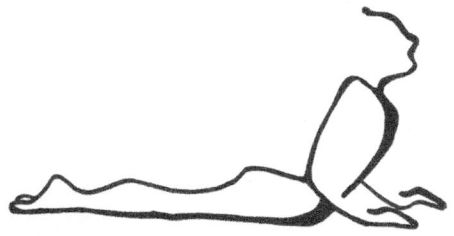

Child

1. From a kneeling position with your hands on your knees, breathe and spread your knees apart, keeping your toes touching.
2. Rest your buttocks on your heels.
3. Sit up straight and stretch your spine.
4. Exhale; bend forward with your chest resting between or on top of your thighs. Let your head touch the floor.
5. Bring your arms back, resting next to your thighs with palms up.
6. Relax your elbows and allow all your tension to fall away.
7. Hold for at least a minute and release gently to a sitting position on your heels.
8. Repeat three to five times.

Locust

1. Lie on your stomach with your arms next to your sides, with your forehead on the mat. Move your hips wide apart and have the tops of your feet touching the mat.

Living from Your Heart The Inner Essence Journey

2. Inhale, raising your head.

3. Exhale, lifting your chest and arms.

4. Lift your upper spine and reach your arms back toward your feet.

5. Lift your legs toward the ceiling. Your weight should rest on your lower ribs and belly.

6. Breathe smoothly and hold up to one minute.

7. Exhale and slowly release your body to the ground. Repeat the pose up to five times and then rest your left ear on the mat.

Corpse

1. Lie on your back.

2. Relax your legs so your feet fall open to either side.

3. Have your arms next to your body (but not touching it).

4. Turn your palms facing up and let your fingers curl in.

5. Relax your whole body (especially your face).

6. Breathe naturally, and if your mind wanders, just bring it back to your breath.

7. Stay for a minimum of three minutes. Set a timer so you don't have to keep looking at the clock. Stay longer if you can.

Third Routine: Listen

Come back to a seated position and close your eyes. For the next minute, sit in silence and listen to the sound of your breath. Focus on your breathing. If your mind is busy and wanders (monkey mind), do not fight it; let the thoughts come and ask them to go.

Fourth Routine: Sing

Chant the sound "Aum" (pronounced *ah-oh-mm*), hum, sigh, or sing a verse from a favorite song. Anything pleasing will help send good vibrations through your body.

CHAPTER 11

Your Chakras

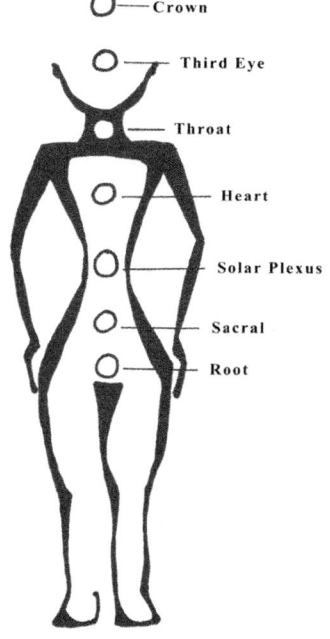

Your body has energy centers, also known as chakras. These are areas in your body that refer to certain critical aspects of your Essence. When you are doing Stop behaviors, the flow of energy through your chakras is blocked, and you feel discomfort or pain in that region of your body. When you are living your Essence, your chakras are clear; the flow of healthy energy and love circulates through your body, and you feel no discomfort. For the sake of consistency, I will call these chakras, but remember, they are also called energy centers. There are seven main chakras: root, sacral, solar plexus, heart, throat, third eye, and crown.

The use of chakras in energetic medicine is fairly recent in the Western world, but practitioners in India, Japan, and China have been using chakras to heal bodies and souls for thousands of years.

Chakras correspond to seven specific energy centers in your physical body. They connect your nerves, hormones, and emotions. They run parallel to your endocrine glands and link your energetic body with your physical body.

Learning about your chakras can help you better understand how energy flows in your body, how emotions contribute to disease, and how food can feed your physical and spiritual bodies. In the following pages, you will learn the location of the chakras in your body and discover which glands are related to which chakra. You will see how the chakras affect your lives.

It is known that certain colors, foods, and gemstones strengthen each chakra. Stephanie Lucas and Quantumstones explain that ancient Egyptians used gemstones and crystals for protection and healing.

The Romans used amulets and crystals for health and protection in battles. From as far back as 5000 years the Chinese have used healing crystals. Azeemi and Raza stated that color medicine (chromotherapy) is as old as any other medicine. The Greeks, Egyptians, Chinese and East Indians used color for healing. Needless to say, we all know how food can heal our bodies.

You will learn what colors and stones to wear if you feel discomfort or an imbalance in a chakra. Finally, you will learn how to recognize when a chakra is not balanced, identify ways to balance it, and help your energy flow smoothly through your body.

Root Chakra

The root chakra, or first chakra, is located at the base of your spine; it establishes the deepest connections with your body and the earth. The root chakra relates to safety, security, and grounding. Your fight-or-flight response is initiated from this chakra. It is your survival center. This chakra is related to your reproductive glands. Practitioners suggest wearing certain colors and gemstones to balance this chakra. The root chakra color is red. Some of the gemstones that relate to this chakra are bloodstone, garnet, ruby, onyx, hematite, and black tourmaline.

If your root chakra is open, you will feel secure in your world and your body. Daily tasks will seem effortless. You will not have any doubts about your place in the world. Relationships, money, and career will flow with ease.

When your root chakra is blocked and out of balance, you might have doubts about your work, daily tasks, relationships, self-worth, and so on. When your root chakra is overactive, you may experience anger, annoyance, and even aggression. You may think that your value or self-worth exists in having material things or certain people in your life. Finally, an overactive sex drive can result from an overactive root chakra. In contrast, if your root chakra is underactive, you may feel disconnected from the world around you and your body. You can feel disorganized, you could lack focus and discipline, and you may even become anxious, afraid, and depressed. An underactive sex drive can occur because of an underactive root chakra.

Some physical symptoms of an out-of-balance root chakra would be fatigue, hemorrhoids, constipation, lower back pain, weight issues, and kidney problems. An imbalanced first chakra can also cause sleep disorders and poor circulation.

If you have any of these symptoms and feel your root chakra is blocked, you should first see if you are doing any Stop behaviors. If so, cease doing them and choose at least one of the five Essential Laws of Life to practice. For example, if you don't feel appreciated at work and think that you will be fired, you are wanting and assuming. You are wanting to feel more appreciative and assuming you'll be fired.

Stop yourself from doing those Stop behaviors. Wear the color red, especially on the lower part of your body, if possible. For example, red underwear, red socks, and red shoes would be good. Wearing a gemstone that pertains to the root chakra can help balance the root chakra. Wear onyx, hematite, or black tourmaline if you feel your root chakra is overactive. Wear ruby, garnet, or bloodstone if you need to open the root chakra. Eat red foods, such as red apples, pomegranates, strawberries, and red cabbage. Ginger, carrots, beets, and foods that are high in protein, such as eggs, meat, beans, and nuts, help balance the root chakra.

This last activity can be used to clear each chakra. Find a quiet place. Light a red candle (if that seems calming) and lie down; focus on the base of the spine and imagine a red wheel spinning in that area. While you are doing this, meditate with the following affirmation: "I am a divine being of light, and I am peaceful, protected, and secure."

Sacral Chakra

The sacral chakra is the second chakra and is located around the spine, two inches below the naval. This chakra is related to creativity, manifestation, relationships, and letting go. It affects your sense of self-worth, confidence in your creativity, and your ability to have healthy relationships. This chakra is related to your adrenal glands and the color orange. The following gemstones pertain to the sacral chakra: ruby, carnelian, citrine, clear quartz, orange calcite, and tiger's eye.

When this chakra is balanced, you feel healthy and strong, physically and emotionally. You are passionate, present in your body, sensual, creative, and connected to your emotions. You experience life through feelings and sensations.

When the sacral chakra is overactive, you tend to be overemotional. You might show signs of sexual addiction, which would show as the Stop behavior wanting. You could have an unhealthy emotional attachment to someone. This would show up in the Stop behavior of holding.

When this chakra is underactive, you might lack creativity. You might have a low sex drive or feel tired and lethargic. You could show fear of pleasures and avoid things that make you feel good.

Signs that the sacral chakra is out of balance include pelvic pain, urinary difficulty, constipation, low back pain, sciatica, and ob/gyn problems. You may feel emotionally explosive, disingenuous, or obsessed with thoughts of sex, or you may lack energy for sex.

To balance the sacral chakra, as with the root chakra, check to see if you are doing any Stop behaviors and abstain from doing them. Then, review and practice the five Laws of Life.

Wearing the color orange and a gemstone that pertains to the sacral chakra can help balance that chakra. Wear ruby, carnelian, citrine, clear quartz, orange calcite, or tiger's eye if you feel your second chakra is blocked. Eating juicy sweet fruits such as oranges, mandarins, and melons, along with almonds and cinnamon, can help with sacral chakra issues.

Follow the meditation routine explained in the root chakra section and imagine a spinning orange wheel over your sacral area. Use an orange candle if you like.

Affirmation: "I am radiant, beautiful, and strong. I am creative, healthy, and passionate." You can also recite this affirmation anytime you feel you need to clear your sacral chakra.

Solar Plexus Chakra

Have you ever had a gut feeling about a situation? Those are the times when you just *know*. You might even sense when something is going to happen. Those feelings truly lie in your gut, the solar plexus area, your third chakra.

The solar plexus is located in the area above the naval and below the ribs. This is the place of personal power, passions, and impulses. This area controls your emotional and mental self as well as your psychic potential. Your willpower comes from this chakra. We all have had that gut feeling, and it is very important to listen to those feelings.

The solar plexus chakra relates to the pancreas and regulates your metabolism. The color for the solar plexus chakra is yellow, and some of the gemstones are jasper, tiger's eye, citrine, yellow tourmaline, malachite, and golden topaz.

When the solar plexus chakra is balanced, you feel accepting of your thoughts and emotions. You will love yourself and others. This love and joy will emanate throughout your body. Others will feel it too.

When your third chakra is overactive, you may blame others and be critical of them. You may have strong emotional challenges. Anger and aggression can arise because of an overactive solar plexus chakra. You can be a workaholic and perfectionist.

When your solar plexus chakra is underactive, you can have doubts and mistrusts. You may spend too much energy monitoring what others think of you, which can be accompanied by low self-concept. You might find yourself avoiding emotions altogether, for fear of what they will bring up. Procrastination can also occur when your solar plexus chakra is underactive.

Physical problems from an out-of-balance third chakra include hypoglycemia, hyperglycemia, anorexia, bulimia, and colon or intestinal problems. Other issues are digestive problems, weight challenges, ulcers, diabetes, pancreatitis, and liver problems.

To balance this chakra, you can, as suggested with the previous chakras, follow these guidelines:

Stop Behaviors: Identify any Stop behaviors to stop.

Essential Laws of Life: Review and practice the Laws of Life. Look specifically at the laws of monitoring and assuming.

Color: Wear yellow; have it around you with yellow flowers and so on.

Gemstones: Jasper, tiger's eye, citrine, yellow tourmaline, malachite, and golden topaz.

Food: Yellow peppers, corn, yellow lentils, yellow curry, and bananas. Grains, granola, sunflower seeds, flax, cheese, and yogurt also help.

Meditation: Spinning yellow wheel over your sacral area with a yellow candle.

Affirmation: "I am confident in all that I do and I trust my own guidance. I am a powerful creator of my life."

The Heart Chakra

The fourth chakra, the heart chakra, connects your body, mind, and spirit. When this chakra is completely open, it becomes a channel of your Essence, your true self. It is the chakra of love and compassion. The heart chakra relates to being able to love yourself and others.

Your heart chakra is in the center of your chest, between your shoulder blades in your back, and behind the breast bone in the front. This chakra affects your heart, lungs, blood, breasts, shoulders, esophagus, arms, and hands.

When your heart chakra is balanced, you feel great love and compassion. You are kind and caring. You exude joyfulness, and others around you can feel it. Your chest area is pain free, and you are completely at peace with who you are.

When this chakra is imbalanced, you may have heart palpitations, blood pressure issues, chest pain, asthma, or poor circulation. In more serious cases, you expose yourself to the possibility of breast cancer or a heart attack. You might feel paranoid, unworthy, angry, or jealous when your heart chakra is imbalanced. Your heart chakra is related to the thymus gland and regulates the immune system.

When the heart chakra is overactive, you can be controlled by your emotions. You might be judgmental of yourself and others. You are probably a people-pleaser if this chakra is overactive.

When this chakra is underactive, you may see the glass as half-empty. It can be very difficult to be positive. You may feel unworthy of love or unappreciated. You may have difficulty trusting others and keep people at a distance.

Use the following guide to balance the heart chakra:

Stop Behaviors: Identify any Stop behaviors to end.

Essential Laws of Life to Practice: Work on the Law of Trust especially if your heart chakra is out of balance.

Color: Green.

Gemstones: Emerald, jade, green aventurine, green tourmaline, rose quartz, and malachite.

Food: Eat green vegetables, such as kale, spinach, greens, broccoli, cabbage, and celery, and drink green teas.

Meditation: Spinning green wheel with green candle.

Affirmation: "I am love, I am peace, I am light."

Throat Chakra

The fifth chakra, the throat chakra, is located in the V of the collarbone and the base of the throat. This chakra affects your communication and lets you express your creativity through speech and writing. This chakra relates to the thyroid gland and regulates body temperature and metabolism. The color for the throat chakra is bright blue.

When your throat chakra is balanced, you may feel centered,

artistic, or musical. You can easily express yourself. You know what you want and are not afraid to ask for it. When you are completely living your Essence, your throat chakra is clear, and you speak your truth.

Physical symptoms of an imbalanced throat chakra are laryngitis, sore throat, gum and tooth issues, ear infections, neck problems, sinus infections, and other throat problems.

When your throat chakra is overactive, you may be overly opinionated and judgmental. You might be verbally abusive. Anger is often stored in the throat.

When your throat chakra is underactive, you may be unable to express yourself; you may hold back or feel timid. You probably have challenges with being honest with yourself. There was a time when my throat chakra was very underactive. I needed to say things that I knew would upset some people. So I didn't say anything. I was doing the Stop behaviors of wanting and assuming. I was wanting them to like me and assuming if I said what I needed to say, they would not. But my body started telling me what I needed to address in order to live closer to my Essence. My voice became very hoarse. At times, I actually lost my voice. Once I had the courage to stop wanting and assuming, I cleared out my throat chakra by saying what I needed to say.

When you feel that your throat chakra is out of balance, you should find time to sit under a blue sky and follow these guidelines:

Stop Behaviors: Discontinue any you are aware of doing.

Essential Laws of Life to Practice: Practicing the Law of Choice and intention often help balance the heart chakra.

Color: Sky blue.

Gemstones: Lapis, blue opal, aquamarine, blue topaz, and blue tourmaline.

Food: Eat foods that are juicy and moist to lubricate this chakra: soups, sauces, and fruits.

Meditation: Light blue spinning wheel with blue candle.

Affirmation: "I hear and speak the truth. I express myself with clear intent. Creativity flows through me. My opinion has value."

Third Eye Chakra

The sixth chakra, the third eye chakra, is also called the brow chakra. Its energy center is located at the center of the forehead. Your insight, ideas, intellect, thoughts, and dreams develop here.

    The color indigo is associated with this chakra. The brain, eyes, ears, nose, pituitary, and pineal glands are regulated by the sixth chakra. The gemstones that relate to the third eye chakra are amethyst, clear quartz, purple fluorite, and lapis.

When the third eye chakra is balanced with the other chakras, you will feel connected to your angels, Higher Self, the Universe, and your God. You can be very intuitive and have a strong memory. You will be able to learn with ease. You will be living your Essence.

When the sixth chakra is imbalanced, you may feel depressed, be afraid of success, or have learning challenges. Physically, an imbalanced third eye chakra can result in migraines, headaches, dizziness, or ear or sinus problems. More serious problems may include brain tumors, strokes, nausea, blindness, deafness, and seizures.

If you have an overactive third eye chakra, you probably will feel stress along with headaches around your temples and forehead. You may be judgmental.

If your third eye chakra is underactive, you often won't be interested in the spiritual side of life, and you may lack empathy. Memory and learning may be difficult.

To balance this chakra, go through the chakra balancing guide:

Stop Behaviors: Identify any Stop behaviors.

Essential Laws of Life to Practice: The Law of Trust is a good one to practice for this chakra.

Color: Wear the color indigo, have it around you with flowers, etc.

Gemstones: Amethyst, clear quartz, purple fluorite, and lapis.

Food: Dark bluish foods like blueberries, red grapes, blackberries, and so on.

Meditation: Indigo spinning wheel with indigo candle.

Affirmation: "I see the beauty of the Universe. I trust my intuition and my dreams. I am clear."

Crown Chakra

The crown chakra relates to spiritual connection located at the top of your head; it is associated with intuition, spirituality, and living in the present. When balanced and aligned with the other chakras, this energy center allows you to live in your complete Essence. With a clear crown chakra, you feel connected with all things and have great compassion for all life. The colors violet and white correspond to the crown chakra. Related gemstones are diamonds, amber, clear quartz, and amethyst. The crown chakra affects your pineal gland and your biological cycles, including sleep.

When this chakra is balanced with the others, you will be very wise and intuitive. You will be aware of your spiritual self.

When your crown chakra is overactive, you can have trouble feeling grounded. You may consider yourself better than others. You could be constantly frustrated and depressed. Physical symptoms of an overactive crown chakra may include feeling unloved and blaming others. Other problems can be migraines, chronic exhaustion, and sensitivity to light and certain sounds.

When your seventh chakra is underactive, you may feel a lack of purpose in life. You may feel unloved and blame others. You may also lack any interest in spiritual exploration and have a great fear of dying.

To balance this chakra, surround yourself with the colors white and violet. You can wear clothes that are those colors and have flowers in your house and workplace that are white or violet. You can wear some of the gemstones that are associated with your crown chakra. The seventh chakra is more spirit than earth, so food cannot balance it. Eating light meals while participating in spiritual activities can help balance your crown chakra.

The most powerful tool to clear your crown chakra is to practice the meditation and affirmation. The spinning wheel can be violet, white, or clear, like a clear crystal or diamond. While you are doing this visualization (or after), you can say the following affirmation: "My spirit is eternal. It loves peace, harmony, and joy. I am open to enlightenment. I am at one with Spirit. I am divinely guided."

Surround yourself with flowers that are the color of the chakra

Living from Your Heart The Inner Essence Journey

you are working on balancing. Also, using the relevant color candle, especially when you are meditating, can help bring that chakra into balance.

Chakra Activity

Look back at some of your Stop behaviors and determine where you felt them in your body. Did they relate to an appropriate chakra? Write them down and the related chakras. The more you practice this, the more you will automatically do it throughout your day.

Stop Behavior   Where Was the Pain?   Chakra

1. Assuming I won't get a certain job   Stomach   Solar plexus
2. _____
3. _____
4. _____
5. _____
6. _____

PART IV
Conclusion

When you end all Stop behaviors and live by the five Essential Laws of Life, your chakras will be balanced and clear. You will be wise and aware of your spiritual self and others. You will truly be living your Essence.

So when you have pain or discomfort in certain areas of your body or you are having unhealthy feelings or thoughts, first look at any Stop behaviors. Cease doing them and choose at least one of the five Essential Laws of Life to practice. Also, look at what part of your body is feeling pain and identify which chakras are affected. Finally, balance and clear those chakras.

The process seems simple, but pursuing your Inner Essence is challenging and requires a commitment to living your Essence as much as you can each day. As you do, you will change. You will have a reverence for yourself and for others, and you will see all the beauty in the world.

Final Note from Katherine

Thank you for reading my book and joining me in creating a more loving and compassionate world. As more and more of us act from our Essence, the world will be a better place.

I am sharing a relatively small amount of information that I feel is helpful and beneficial about stretching, breathing, and your chakras. If you are interested in knowing more about yoga and other techniques to help your body stay healthy and balanced, search the Internet, go to your local bookstore, or go to a local yoga studio. There is so much information about chakras on the Internet. Please check it out to learn more if that interests you. There are some suggested readings in the back of this book.

Your Inner Essence Journey is a lifetime practice. Each day, you will be faced with urges to do Stop behaviors, and each day you will work on following the five Essential Laws of Life and resisting those Stop behaviors. I recommend journaling to support your Inner Essence Journey. We are on this journey together. If you want individual support with your Inner Essence, you can contact me at theessenceproject@gmail.com. I'll see you on the path to love and compassion.

Namaste, Katherine

History of the Inner Essence Journey

My colleague Kelly Rettig and I concluded that schools and classrooms need a foundation of love and compassion in order to make them a successful community. The Inner Essence Project was created.

The Inner Essence Project for Classrooms (IEPC) helps students, teachers, and families increase their self-awareness and the power of choice. This project encourages students to reach their emotional, physical, and academic potential.

The purpose of the IEPC is to create a sustainable, energy-based practice that nurtures the emotional growth of children and adults within the classroom, at school, and in the home. It is a compassionate program that positively impacts the cooperative skills of students and the adults who serve them.

The program increases self-awareness in the power of choice. It uses a language to teach students and adults how to identify healthy choices (those that serve them well) and unhealthy choices (behaviors that create suffering within themselves and others). It also teaches the pointlessness and harmfulness of judgments. The students and teachers learn the Stop behaviors that come from unhealthy parts of our personality and the five Essential Laws of Life, which they refer to when needing to make healthier choices. Ultimately, the IEPC instills life-sustaining skills in participants that will ultimately have a positive effect on their lives.

Seeing the positive effects the Inner Essence Project for Classrooms had on students was expected. However, witnessing the positive effects the project had on students, parents, and teachers was not anticipated and was a powerful secondary finding. As a result, the Inner Essence Journey was created.

PART V
Affirmations, Quotes, and Prayers

Affirmations

"I am enough."

—Louise Hay

"I accept my life as it is. I do not judge; I do not dramatize. I let life's events come freely and I welcome the lessons they convey. I stop struggling now. I let go and know that God always gives me that which is most appropriate for my soul."

—Author unknown

"I renounce all assumptions and expectations."

—Author unknown

"Note to self: I am doing the best that I can with what I have in this moment. And that is all I can expect of anyone, including me."

—Author unknown

"I release the inclination to make anyone else wrong."
—Author unknown

"I let go of my assumptions and can clearly see the truth in my experiences!
I release stress for what it is, false assumptions!
I let go of the negative assumptions I have about myself.
I give thanks that this or something better is in the Divine flow of my life and is manifesting perfectly for me now according to the Divine will of [the Universe]."
—K.G. Stiles

"I am visualizing my intended outcome. (Then do it.)"
—Author unknown

"I choose to make the rest of my life the best of my life."
—Louise Hay

"Today is a good day and I can do this."
—Louise Hay

"I thoughtfully consider all possibilities, and CHOOSE among them with consciousness."
—Jonathan Lockwood Huie

"I am a magnificent being with an abundance of power and love to give."
—Author unknown

"Everything I give to others is a gift to myself. As I give, I receive."

—*Author unknown*

"I trust in divine timing, the Universe always has my back."
—*Sarah Prout*

"Everything that I need comes to me at the perfect time."
—*Louise Hay*

"I am in the right place at the right time, doing the right thing."

—*Louise Hay*

"I am present within myself. I can center myself with the ease of my breath. I feel grounded, confident, worthy and whole."
—*Author unknown*

Katherine A. Dasta

Five Daily Reminders

1. *I am amazing.*
2. *I can do anything.*
3. *Positivity is a choice.*
4. *I celebrate my individuality.*
5. *I am prepared to succeed.*

"I am a magnet for miracles."

—Louise Hay

Quotes and Prayers

"It is never too late to change the direction that your life is going in.

—Wayne Dyer

"Have faith in your journey. Everything had to happen exactly as it did to get you where you're going next."

—Mandy Hale

*"Don't change so people will like you.
Be yourself and the right people will
love the real you."*

—Author unknown

*"Dear Past,
Thank you for all the lessons.
Dear Future,
I am ready."*

—Author unknown

*"Your future is created by what you do
TODAY not tomorrow."*

—Author unknown

"The longest journey you will make in your life is from your head to your heart."

—Gary Zukav

"Your thoughts not the world cause your stress."
—Wayne Dyer

"Needing nothing attracts everything."
—Author unknown

"It's not how much we give but how much love we put into giving."
—Saint Teresa

When Socrates was asked if he wanted to know what people were saying about him, he said to "filter everything you say through three sieves. #1. Truth: Are you sure what you are about to say is true? #2. Good: Do you want to say something that is good? #3. Useful: Do I really need to hear what you want to say? If you say no to any of these, why bother saying it?"

"If you believe it will work out, you'll see opportunities. If you believe it won't, you will see obstacles."
—Wayne Dyer

"The light of God surrounds [me, us, name].
The love of God enfolds me.
The health of God flows through me.
The power of God protects me.
The presence of God watches over me.
Wherever [we are, I am, name is] God is and all is well!"
—James Freeman

"God grant me the serenity to accept the things I cannot change, the courage to change the things I can and the wisdom to know the difference."

—Reinhold Neibuhr

"May all beings have happiness and its causes.
May all beings be freed from suffering and its causes.
May all beings constantly dwell in joy transcending sorrow.
May all beings dwell in equal love for those both close and distant."

—Buddhist prayer

SUGGESTED READING

Choquette, Sonia. *Your 3 Best Super Powers: Meditation, Imagination & Intuition.* Hay House, 2016.

Gilbert, Elizabeth. *Big Magic.* Penguin Group, 2015.

Grout, Pam. *E-Cubed: Nine More Energy Experiments That Prove Manifesting Magic and Miracles Is Your Full-Time Gig.* Hay House, 2014.

Hay, Louise. *You Can Heal Your Life.* Hay House, 1984.

Hay, Louise. *The Power Is within You.* Hay House, 1991.

Judith, Anodea. *Chakras: Seven Keys to Awakening and Healing the Energy Body.* Hay House, 2016.

Maltz, Maxwell. *Psycho-Cybernetics: Updated and Expanded.* TarcherPerigee, 2015.

Morello, Tai. *The Yoga Beginner's Bible: Top 57 Illustrated Poses for Weight Loss, Stress Relief and Inner Peace.* CreateSpace Independent Publishing Platform, 2016.

Yamashita, Alexander. *Yoga for Beginners: Your Guide to Master Yoga Poses while Calming Your Mind, to be Stress Free, and Boost Your Self-Esteem!* CreateSpace Independent Publishing Platform, 2015.

Zukav, Gary. *The Seat of the Soul: 25th Anniversary Edition with a Study Guide.* Simon and Schuster, 2014.

NOTES:

NOTES:

NOTES:

NOTES:

NOTES:

NOTES:

NOTES:

NOTES:

NOTES:

NOTES:

NOTES:

NOTES:

ABOUT THE AUTHOR

Katherine Dasta is a co-founder of the Inner Essence Project. She has written several curricula for children and adults and has taught a range of ages and subjects. She continues to practice living from her Essence and supports others on their Essence journey. Katherine lives in Florida writing and enjoying her family.

Printed in Dunstable, United Kingdom